Up in the air

Written by Gill Munton

Speed Sounds

Consonants   *Ask children to say the sounds.*

f	l	m	n	r	s	v	z	sh	**th**	**ng**
ff	ll	mm	nn	rr	ss	ve	zz			nk
	le		kn		se		se			
					ce		s			

b	c	d	g	h	j	p	qu	t	w	x	y	ch
bb	k	dd	gg		j	pp		tt	**wh**			tch
	ck				g							
					ge							

Each box contains one sound but sometimes more than one grapheme.
*Focus graphemes for this story are **circled**.*

Vowels

Ask children to say the sounds in and out of order.

a	e ea	i	o	u	ay	ee y	igh	ow
at	hen	in	on	up	day	see	high	blow

oo	oo	ar	or oor ore	air	ir	ou	oy
zoo	look	car	for	fair	whirl	shout	boy

Story Green Words

Ask children to read the words first in Fred Talk and then say the word.

air   flap   gas   lit   send   pull   cord   top
wind   hair

Ask children to say the syllables and then read the whole word.

ba|lloon   bas|ket   be|low

Ask children to read the root first and then the whole word with the suffix.

hang → hangs   jet → jets   light → lighter
pass → passes   blow → blows

Vocabulary Check

Discuss the meaning (as used in the non-fiction text) after the children have read the word.

	definition
gas	gas is like air, but you can burn it to make heat
jets	streams of gas that are lit to create the flame
flap	a part of something that can be moved to make a hole
cord	a thin rope

Red Words

Ask children to practise reading the words across the rows, down the columns and in and out of order clearly and quickly.

you	are	of	so
goes	into	above	to
go	your	the	there
who	what	water	come

This is a hot air balloon. You sit in a basket that hangs below the balloon.

G-BUKC

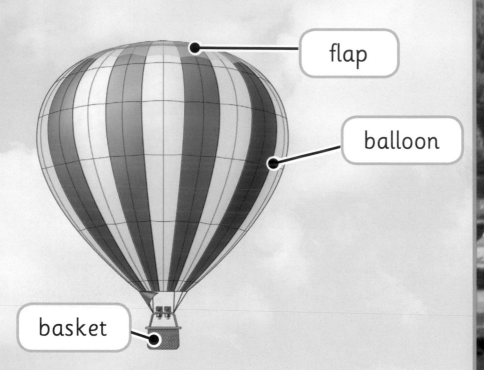

flap

balloon

basket

When the gas jets are lit, the air gets hot. Hot air is lighter than cool air, so the hot air goes up into the balloon.

Then the balloon goes up, high above the trees.

To go higher, you send up more hot air.

hot air

To go lower, you pull a cord. This pulls back a flap at the top of the balloon.

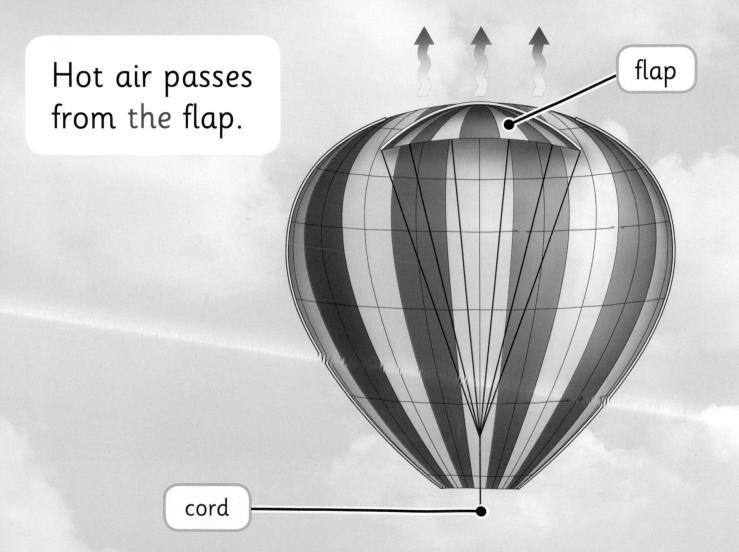

Hot air passes from the flap.

flap

cord

The wind blows the balloon left and right.

It blows your hair, too!

16

Questions to talk about

Ask children to TTYP for each question using 'Fastest finger' (FF) or 'Have a think' (HaT).

p.9 (FF) What hangs under the balloon?

p.10 (FF) What happens when the gas jets are lit?

p.12 (FF) What do you do to make a hot air balloon go higher?

p.14 (HaT) What does pulling the cord do to the height of the balloon?

p.16 (FF) Where does the wind blow the balloon?

Questions to read and answer

(Children complete without your help.)

1. A basket hangs **above** / **below** / **in** the balloon.

2. The balloon goes high above the **trees** / **cars** / **pond**.

3. If you want to go down you pull a **flap** / **cord** / **jet**.

4. The wind blows the balloon from left to **right** / **top** / **below**.

5. The **balloon** / **flap** / **wind** blows your hair too.